HOW DID THEY BUILD THAT?

Guggenheim Museum

MICHELLE LEE

How Did They Build That? Guggenheim Museum

Scobre Educational
2255 Calle Clara
La Jolla, CA 92037

Scobre Operations & Administration
42982 Osgood Road
Fremont, CA 94539

www.scobre.com
info@scobre.com

Scobre Educational publications may be purchased for
educational, business, or sales promotional use.

Cover design by Sara Radka
Layout design by Nicole Ramsay
Photos thanks to Newscom, iStockPhoto, and Shutterstock

ISBN: 978-1-62920-564-9 (Library Bound)
ISBN: 978-1-62920-563-2 (eBook)

INDEX

INTRODUCTION

The Guggenheim Museum Bilbao is a museum unlike any other. When people go to a museum, they're usually interested in what's *inside* it, but this one is beautiful both inside and out. Built along the waters of Bilbao, Spain, the museum is a peaceful building that blends into its **environment**. It is covered in bright silver metal that changes color depending on the weather and time of day. In the sun, the building has a golden orange glow, while at night, the moonlight reflects a calm and cool blue.

The Guggenheim Museum is located along the Nervión River in Bilbao, Spain.

The museum uses modern **architecture** and is built in a style called **deconstructivism**. Deconstructing something means taking it apart. Instead of building a normal **structure** that is perfectly straight and balanced, **architect** Frank Gehry took that idea apart and created something new and exciting.

Removing many of the straight edges of the building, we are left with naturally round and curving shapes. The top of the museum has many wavy layers, reminding people of the waves that move just beneath the building.

In fact, the design of the building is made to look like a giant ship. The museum is located in a port city that depends on ships for its business, so Gehry wanted to make a building to reflect Bilbao's people and culture.

The inside of the museum is just as impressive. The most interesting part is the **Atrium**, a great entrance hall with a domed window at the top. The Atrium is surrounded by three floors that lead to rooms filled with modern paintings, drawings, sculptures, and **exhibitions**. The art is made by native Spanish artists and others from around the world.

DID YOU KNOW?
The people of Bilbao call the Guggenheim Museum "the artichoke" because of its unique shape.

HISTORY

The Guggenheim Museum Bilbao is part of four museums that belong to the Solomon R. Guggenheim Foundation. This **foundation** is dedicated to collecting, studying, and protecting modern and **contemporary** art. The other three Guggenheim museums are in New York City, Venice, and Abu Dhabi.

Bilbao is located in the Basque country of Spain and the Basque people were responsible for the building of the museum. At the time, Bilbao was a city that was not doing well **economically**. There were few jobs and nothing that really made the city a desirable place to go to. It was mainly a working town filled with factories and ship ports—not a place known for its beauty or art.

However, the Basque people wanted to change this. They wanted to make something that would prove to the world just how wrong it was. Bilbao was a beautiful place with a rich culture and history and so the Guggenheim Museum was created in order to showcase the city and country's many talents.

Bilbao is a port city that earns its wealth from the ship trade along its waters.

Even the design of the building reflects the people's pride in their city. When Gehry was hired to build the museum, he made sure that the building highlighted the beauty of Bilbao that was already there. Since Bilbao is a river city, he decided to add elements of the environment into the design.

The titanium steel that covers the museum changes color just like a river does when reflecting the colors of the sky. The building is shaped like a boat and is poised on the edge of the river as if it is ready to sail away. The part of the building that faces the river has a smooth sleek side like the scales of a fish while the other side has a stone and brick design that blends with the other buildings of the city. The Guggenheim Museum Bilbao is just like a mermaid—half fish and half human. One side is connected to the water while the other side stays connected to the land.

After the Basque government gained permission to build the museum, the Solomon R. Guggenheim Foundation agreed to run the museum, add art from its own collection, and organize temporary exhibitions and shows. Each month has special galleries that feature different artists and their work.

In order to use the world-famous Guggenheim name, the Basque government paid a $20 million fee and agreed to pay for all the costs of the building. **Construction** began in October 1993 and only took four years to complete. What is even more surprising is how cheap it was to make it. The government had $100 million set aside for the museum but the construction was so well done that they did not have to use all the money. This is all because of the architect Frank Gehry—whose careful planning and hard work saved the Basque people millions of dollars and valuable time.

The front entrance of the museum

The building of the Guggenheim Museum also went through many changes. Gehry constantly drew and redrew the design of the building—going over at least 100 different drafts and sketches before starting construction. At first, the Atrium was supposed to be shaped like a flower with rooms that curved around the center like petals. However, the museum director, Thomas Krens, thought the design was too common and so they worked together to come up with a more interesting and unique design. Eventually, Gehry decided to make the roof of the building look like a metal flower from above. Called a masterpiece of the 20th century, the museum was opened to the public by Spain's Queen Sofia and King Juan Carlos I in 1997.

DID YOU KNOW?

The museum is very popular. It was featured in the James Bond film, The World is Not Enough (1999) as well as Mariah Carey's music video for "Sweetheart." The museum was also the location for concerts by Smashing Pumpkins and the Red Hot Chili Peppers. You can even build the museum in the SimCity 4 game.

The top of the museum looks like a large, metal flower.

Guggenheim Museum Bilbao

TIMELINE

The Construction Timeline of the Guggenheim Museum Bilbao

1992　　1993　　1994

EARLY 1990s
After winning an architectural competition, Frank Gehry is chosen to be the museum's architect. Because the design of the building has many curves and twists that are difficult to measure and calculate by hand, Gehry uses an advanced computer program called CATIA to calculate the exact measurements as well as a 3-D model of the structure.

1993
Construction of the museum begins. The first step of building is creating the foundation. The land is flattened out and topped with limestone.

1993-1994
Next, a 5,000-ton steel frame is built on top of the foundation.

1994
The bones of the structure are covered with a titanium metal skin.

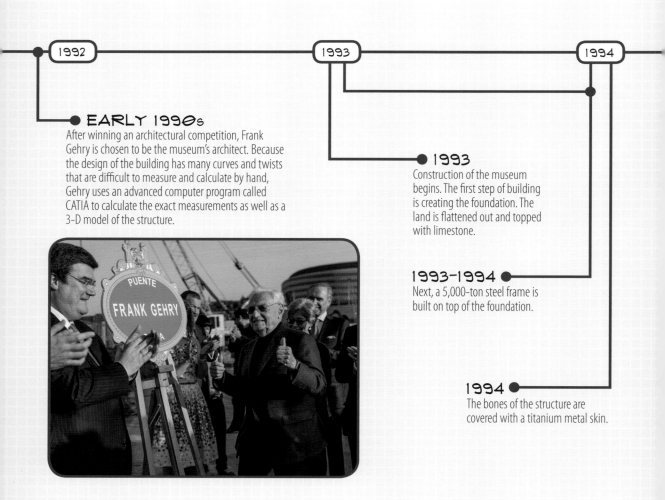

1995–1997
Work is done on the inside of the building. Walls, windows, and doors are installed.

1995   1996   1997

1995
The curved roofs are made and placed on top of the steel frame.

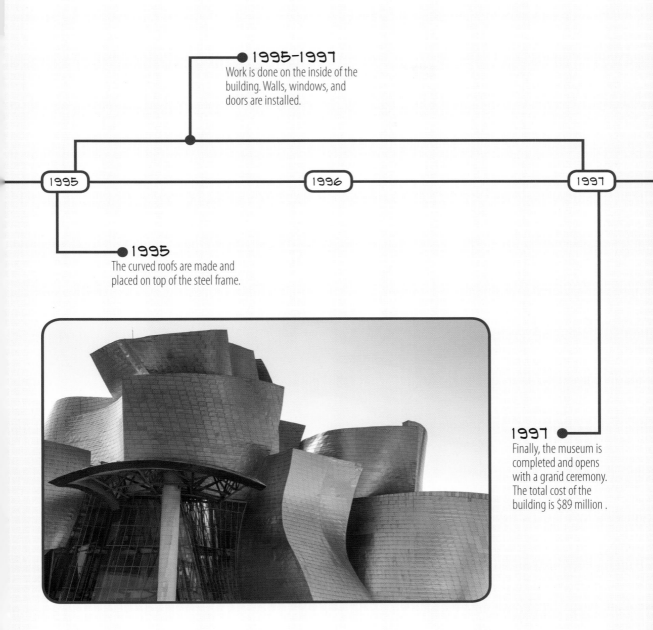

1997
Finally, the museum is completed and opens with a grand ceremony. The total cost of the building is $89 million .

LOCATION

The Guggenheim Museum Bilbao is located in Bilbao, Basque country, Spain. Before the building was created, Bilbao was an industrial city. In the 19th century, the area was rich in iron ore and Bilbao soon became a leader in steel production.

Many factories filled up the town and ships were constantly coming and going in order to supply the people's demand for steel. However, towards the 20th century, people began turning to other places for steel and the city lost a major source of its income.

The factories were closed down and many ships stayed in their harbors as they had nothing more to carry

Despite being an industrial city, Bilbao is still home to many charming waterside buildings.

and sell. This caused great unemployment in the city. Few people visited Bilbao and many businesses struggled without customers. To save Bilbao, the Basque government decided to renew the city and make it more attractive to visitors.

This led to the building of more arts and cultural centers, the most famous being the Guggenheim Museum. Now a million people visit Bilbao each year, bringing jobs and businesses back into full swing. Bilbao has successfully changed from a dying, factory town into a beautiful and lively city.

DID YOU KNOW?
Bilbao is an old city that has been around since the 1300s.

PURPOSE

The Guggenheim Museum Bilbao is responsible for two important things: protecting art and teaching others about the value of culture, history, and human expression. **Art conservators** make sure that all of the art in the museum is taken care of. They are in charge of transporting and storing art safely, and repainting or restoring art pieces that have been damaged from old age. Their duty is to save art for future generations to study and enjoy.

In the museum, there are tour guides who help visitors find their way. Their job is to answer questions and explain the meaning behind each art piece.. Their job is to answer questions, tell people a little bit about the artist and materials used, as well as the importance of the culture and history behind the work. The Guggenheim Museum Bilbao is a good place to explore new worlds, cultures, and experiences as seen through the eyes of many unique artists.

The Guggenheim Museum Bilbao has many different kinds of art both inside and outside, such as this giant puppy sculpture made of flowers.

MATERIALS

The Guggenheim Museum Bilbao is made mostly from limestone, glass, steel, and titanium. The limestone is used for the foundation and to make some of the building's towers. It is also used for the walls of public areas such as the restaurants and bookstore. The limestone was chosen because it is a very strong and solid material. The glass is used for the windows. At the entrance of the museum, there is a giant glass wall as well as a domed glass window at the top of the Atrium.

The steel is used as the framework of the building. It preserves the shape and supports the weight of the building. Titanium is

The museum's metal walls are built on top of a strong limestone base.

The titanium tiles that cover the museum were made to look like fish scales.

used to cover the outside of the building. It was chosen because it is a lighter and cheaper material than steel. The metal also has a sleek and smoother look and is **weatherproof**. Titanium also reflects light and changes into different colors throughout the day. The reflection of light is also important because it prevents sun glare. While the building is shiny, it is not too bright to distract drivers or hurt people's eyes.

DID YOU KNOW?
To create the building's curved glass windows, the glass was cut into triangles instead of rectangles.

FEATURES

The building is memorable and unique for many reasons. The first reason is for its new and daring architecture. Using deconstructivism, Gehry chose a design that goes against the normal style of other buildings. It is irregular in shape—a mix and match of stone, glass, and metal. On one side it looks like an ordinary building, but on the riverside, it looks like a ship with strange and fantastical sculptures around it.

The second reason the building is famous is because it is a world-class museum. There are only three other Guggenheim museums in the world. The Bilbao museum is filled with different kinds of art and exhibitions. It is also a contemporary museum, so it includes not only paintings and drawings, but new forms of art like digital and video material. It is a very advanced museum that contains art from many famous artists such as Antoni Tapies, Eduardo Chillida, Andy Warhol, Richard Serra, Yves Klein, Louise Bourgeois, and Daniel Buren.

The museum features modern and futuristic art, such as this blue light sculpture by native Spanish artist Eduardo Chillida.

HIGHLIGHTS

THE MATTER OF TIME

The Matter of Time (1994) is a famous series of sculptures that is on display in the Guggenheim Museum Bilbao. Created by artist Richard Serra, the exhibition is made up of eight different steel sculptures. They are round or spiraling pathways that viewers can walk through. Some paths are wide, some are narrow, some are long or short, tall or low. Serra wanted people to feel as if they are travelling through time as they walk through his sculptures.

FIRE FOUNTAIN

The Fire Fountain (1961) is an exhibition by the artist Yves Klein. It is a row of fire flames that stands in front of the entrance to the Guggenheim Museum Bilbao. When Klein saw the grand fountains of the Royal Palace of La Granja de San Ildefonso in Spain, he imagined replacing the jets of water with fire. It was his dream to create a fire fountain in front of a grand building. However, Klein died before he could see it come true. In his honor, the *Fire Fountain* was made and placed in front of the world-famous museum.

MAMAN

Maman (1999) is a spider sculpture by Louise Bourgeois. It is made of bronze, marble, and steel, and stands near a walking bridge that leads to the entrance of the museum. *Maman* is the French word for mother, and the sculpture is all about mothers. The sculpture was made in honor of Bourgeois's mother, who was a weaver. Bourgeois saw spiders as symbols of motherhood because of how protective they are of their young. Mother spiders wrap many layers of silk around their eggs to keep them safe. Then they guard their egg sacs and wait for them to hatch. Bourgeois's sculpture mimics this interesting spider behavior.

ARCOS ROJOS / ARKU GORRIAK

Arcos rojos / Arku gorriak is a structure created by Daniel Buren. It is made of aluminum, steel, and Plexiglas, and is located on a bridge near the Guggenheim Museum. To celebrate the museum's 10th anniversary, Buren was set with the task of making the La Salve Bridge more noticeable. He decided to add a large red arch to the top of the bridge. The arch was created by taking a long piece of metal and cutting out a circle in the middle and two semi-circles on each end. The bottom semi-circle arches over the water while the top semi circle curves up towards the sky. The circle at the middle allows cars to drive through the bridge.

SIMILAR STRUCTURES

GUGGENHEIM MUSEUM
NEW YORK, UNITED STATES

This is the first museum that was created by the Solomon R. Guggenheim Foundation. It is a building that is shaped like an orange fruit and divided into many floors. Unlike most museums, the New York Guggenheim starts at the top. Visitors can take an elevator and then look at art as they slowly walk down a spiraling ramp.

GUGGENHEIM MUSEUM
VENICE, ITALY

The Guggenheim Museum is located in an 18th century palace along Venice's Grand Canal. It is one of Italy's most famous museums and features American and European Art from the 20th century. It contains masterpieces by artists such as Pablo Picasso, Salvador Dalí, and Gino Severini.

HO

GUGGENHEIM MUSEUM ABU DHABI, UNITED ARAB EMIRATES

The Guggenheim Museum Abu Dhabi is currently in the process of construction; however, it is also being designed by the world-famous architect, Frank Gehry. He plans to make the building a mix between ancient Arabian and modern architecture. The museum will be dedicated to contemporary Middle Eastern art!

WALT DISNEY CONCERT HALL, LOS ANGELES, CALIFORNIA

After finishing the Guggenheim Museum Bilbao, many people were impressed with Gehry's work and wanted him to make the Walt Disney Concert Hall. At first, Gehry planned to make the building out of stone, but the success of Bilbao made him turn to metal instead. As a result, the building looks very similar with its shining, silver sails.

PEOPLE

Frank Gehry is the main architect of the Guggenheim Museum Bilbao. He has achieved much worldwide fame for his unique and out of the ordinary designs. Most of his work is inspired by nature and the environment around him. He likes the freedom that natural shapes have rather than the straight lines and squares of other buildings.

Gehry's creativity has led him to many other strange designs. For example, he helped design the "Dancing House" in Prague, a building that looks like two

Frank Gehry, the man who created Guggenheim Museum Bilbao.

people dancing. He also designed the house he lives in. After buying a pink house, he took parts out of it and replaced it with glass, allowing some parts of his house to be visible. The strange design angered a lot of his neighbors, but it inspired Gehry to keep doing his own style even if it did not please everyone. Eventually, his boldness paid off and people grew to love the pink house. It is now a famous tourist sight.

DID YOU KNOW?
Gehry even designed a hat for Lady Gaga.

IMPACT

With a million visitors each year, the Guggenheim Museum Bilbao is a very popular destination. Any time of the year is a good time to visit. Visitors will enter a welcome room, learn about what the museum has to offer, and may join a tour if they wish. The museum has a permanent collection of art available for viewing all the time, but it also has special exhibitions that are only available for a limited time each month, so visitors can always see something new.

The museum also brings great wealth to Bilbao. Within just three years of its opening, Bilbao and the Basque country saw a rise in visitors and earned $455 million. The money was used to improve the city and make new businesses, homes, and schools. Many people were amazed by Bilbao's sudden improvement and called this event the "Guggenheim Effect." Once a city on the brink of financial ruin, Bilbao is now blooming with life. The museum is a building that both lives and breathes art. If not admiring the building itself, visitors can admire the many wonders that are hidden inside.

The Guggenheim Museum Bilbao at night

GLOSSARY

architect: a person who designs buildings and other structures

architecture: the art or style of a building

art conservator: someone whose job is to protect art

atrium: a large hall that usually has many floors and a glass roof at the top

construction: the process of building something

contemporary: an adjective used to describe something from the present time (now)

deconstructivism: architecture that does not use normal geometric shapes like squares, triangles, or circles

economically: in a way that involves money; used to describe the wealth of a person, city, country, etc.

environment: the outside elements or natural surroundings

exhibition: the public display of an artist's work

foundation: the ground on which a building stands; or an organization that helps the arts

structure: something that is built or constructed, like a building, house, or bridge

weatherproof: something that can survive the elements of the weather without being damaged